Dropshipping

Discover How to Create an Online
Dropshipping Business, Select a Niche and
Source a Good Supplier - All in One Day

"The World Is Yours"

Max Armin

Dropshipping

Discover How to Create an Online Dropshipping Business, Select a Niche and Source a Good Supplier – All In One Day

Furthermore, the transmission, duplication or reproduction of any of the following work including specific information will be considered an illegal act irrespective of if it is done electronically or in print. This extends to creating a secondary or tertiary copy of the work or a recorded copy and is only allowed with express written consent from the Publisher. All additional rights reserved.

The information in the following pages is broadly considered to be a truthful and accurate account of facts and as such any inattention, use or misuse of the information in question by the reader will render any resulting actions solely under their purview. There are no scenarios in which the publisher or the original author of this work can be in any fashion deemed liable for any hardship or damages that may befall them after undertaking information described herein. Additionally, the information in the following pages is intended only for informational purposes and should thus be thought of as universal. As befitting its nature, it is presented without assurance regarding its prolonged validity or interim quality. Trademarks that are mentioned are done without written consent and can in no way be considered an endorsement from the trademark holder.

Table of Contents

Introduction to Dropshipping

Hello, my name's Max and I have been an Internet marketer since 1998. I'm old school, and I have seen this "Internet wave" grow beyond what everyone thought it would ever be. When I started, it was a lot harder than it is now to set up an online business. I personally started in the affiliate marketing business by selling electronic books and reports through a couple static HTML websites that I built and maintained. Back then everyone focused on SEO listings and link exchanges instead of paid ads. Things are much different now, SEO is a lot tougher, and most successful affiliate marketers now use online paid ads (such as; Pay-per-click, Display ads, YouTube ads, FaceBook ads, Bing ads, and other less known CPA networks) for driving traffic and conversions. Plus, Google being the dominant search engine now, options are limited to their algorithms for SEO to work with your website, especially if Google doesn't like your website.

Back in the early days of Internet marketing, I had to work 14 hour days because we had to make and publish our own websites from basic HTML code and FTP utilities. BUT, SEO was extremely easy and getting traffic was literally as simple as pushing a button, it was easy to make money because the search engines back then were way different than now.

You could also spam the Internet back then and make money from selling information products via email based on a numbers formula, for example; you could broadcast 2 million emails using bulk email software and "farmed" email lists and get a .08% - 1% response rate that would buy the info product you were selling. Obviously this is no longer feasible, but in retrospect, anyone starting today has it a lot better, in my opinion.

The tools and software's available to online entrepreneurs make the logistics very easy now, and data analytics have changed the whole game. So, now really is the best time ever to get into this business, ecommerce is still maturing, but very quickly; so eventually down the road there will be more changes and consolidation. Why wait? Start your dream today; you are in the right place at the right time!

Increasing in popularity and growing in demand, ecommerce dropshipping has become big business. Why? Simply because of the many benefits that this business model brings. Possibly one of the best things about the dropshipping business is that it eliminates the need to take stock or keep any inventory of any sort for the items that you plan to sell.

That's right; all you're going to need is an e-commerce website and a strong internet connection. In this book, you'll learn the basic foundations you'll need to start a successful dropshipping business for yourself. Like any business model, getting started on the right foot is going to be the essential driving force of your success. Too many entrepreneurs that start off incorrectly with the wrong strategy lose enthusiasm and persistence really fast. The dropshipping industry is a competitive one, and to stand out from your competitors, you're going to have to work hard and be creative to stand out from your competitors. There are many things you will have to master, marketing being one of them. Marketing is a pre-requisite no matter what business you go into, so let's get that fact cleared up front. In addition, you have to be in a good niche and not waste your money in a niche that is very hard to profit from, for a beginner. Also, remember that just because you are starting an Internet business does not mean it will be easy because you can do this from home using websites and images. Mental work and creativity is just as hard as running a brick and mortar storefront, sometimes harder.

As you get deep into your online dropshipping store, you will realize this. The key to overcoming "Internet Fatigue" is to take breaks, it sounds simple but it's the only way to overcome it. When you mind goes blank or you cannot find the energy to keep working, take a break for a few hours, or even a whole day. Do anything but work on your business. When you go back, you will be refreshed and full of ideas.

This book contains the simple information that you need to start, build and run your store, but it's also going to let you know how to *keep* your store running by avoiding the common mistakes. One of these common mistakes involves picking the wrong supplier for your business. As you continue on you will discover just how crucial suppliers can be to your business model.

Chapter 1: Dropshipping Defined

So you've made a decision to become an e-commerce entrepreneur? Venturing out on your own, attempting to build your own business empire, no matter how small or big, is a great achievement to be proud of. You never know where a new opportunity is going to lead you, and that's one of the best things about the Internet business world. Everyday brings the possibility of something new very fast.

What's even better about dropshipping is that you don't *need* to keep stock or inventory of the items that you intend to sell. You don't need to keep stock or inventory the way you would have to with a regular retail business.

Dropshipping, as you will quickly discover, the one of the easiest businesses in the e-commerce world that you could start out with. It may be easy, but it is also profitable. If you're starting out without a lot of capital to play around with, then this is the perfect business for you to get started with.

Let's begin by first defining what the dropshipping business is all about.

Dropshipping Defined

Dropshipping is part of the retail world. In the retail model, it is a defined as a store which allows you to sell merchandise and products *but without* physically holding onto any of the inventory. This means that you don't physically keep the products with you on hand or in stock. This effectively eliminates the need for you to have your own brick and mortar store to keep stock of these items, or even the need to rent a warehouse where you'd need to keep these products until a customer orders them.

With dropshipping, when a customer orders a product, what happens is that the seller will then purchase the item from a third party vendor. The merchant will not be directly handling or seeing the product in question. This third-party vendor is then responsible for shipping the item directly to the customer. Third-party suppliers focus on manufacturing or wholesaling. This retail partner effectively works together with the dropship supplier which does the manufacturing, warehousing, packaging, and shipping of these products on behalf of the retailer.

To sum it up, here is how dropshipping works in a nutshell:

- The customer makes an order for a product seen on the merchant's online store.
- The merchant records the order purchase. Next, these details get automatically sent to the dropship supplier, complete with order details and customer information.
- The dropship supplier will then work on packaging the products before shipping it out according to the information provided by the customer.

Are There Pros and Cons to Dropshipping?

Yes, like everything else, there most certainly are pros and cons that come with every business. Even the easy ones like dropshipping. Dropshipping is a retail model which is unlike any other. There is one, very defining difference, which sets it apart from all the other business models, and that is the fact that the retail owner does not own any stock or inventory of the items that they intend to sell. With dropshipping, the merchant does something a little different. They only order the inventory if and when there is a need for it (when a sale has been made).

Why dropshipping has become such an appealing business model, especially for those who do not have the benefit of having a big funding source to start with at the beginning. Eliminating the need for a physical office space, or the cost of having to rent a warehouse will cut your business cost significantly, saving you tons of money. With dropshipping, all you will need is an internet connection, and a website where you can directly upload and store information about your products or services.

The other benefits that come with dropshipping include:

- Setting up a dropshipping business is extremely easy when compared to setting up a physical business or retail space.
- Dropshipping businesses only involve three steps, which are

finding a supplier, setting up a website and listing the products or services that you intend to sell.

- Dropshipping is easy to understand and implement, as you will quickly discover by the end of this book.
- It will cost you literally next to nothing to set up a dropshipping business. It eliminates the need for the conventional costs which come with a regular business, including rental, the cost of running your operations, employing staff, paying utility bills and more.
- The only costs involved with running a dropshipping business is the cost of running your website, your domain name registration and the cost of hosting themes. Oh, and your internet cost of course.
- Dropshipping does not involve any high overhead costs either.
- The risks involved with dropshipping are significantly lower, since there is no pressure to sell the inventory as fast as possible when you're not physically holding onto the stock.
- You have the benefit of running your business from anywhere in the world, as long as you have a strong internet connection on your side. This means you could run your business from literally anywhere you may be. In a coffee shop, by the beach, in the comfort of your own home. Anywhere. That's one perk you'll be hard pressed to find with a lot of jobs.
- There is a dropshipping supplier available for just about any type of product.

- You don't have to be confined to selling just one product with dropshipping. You could choose to sell one, two or even a mix of several products if you'd like.

- Dropshipping leaves you with more time to look into finding more resources to scale your business.

- You will not have to put a large amount of investment into your business from the very beginning, the way that you would with a traditional brick and mortar business. Of course, there is going to be some initial cost involved, but the amount is significantly more manageable that a conventional business model.

- It minimizes the losses incurred from damaged goods. Goods are sent directly from the supplier to the customer, and with less shipping steps involved, the risk of items being lost in shipment or damaged is significantly reduced.

The disadvantages of a dropshipping business, however, include the following:

- The profit margins are going to be slightly lower with dropshipping businesses. That's because, depending on your niche market, dropshipping suppliers may charge you higher prices based on where your niche market is located and what they require. This is turn, is going to impact how much profit you're going to make per sale if you have to factor in those additional costs.

- Another downside to this business is that you will have to bear the responsibility and be liable if anything were to go wrong. Even if the fault lies with the supplier, because the customers are making a purchase *from your website*. If the supplier fails to fulfil their end of the bargain, the customer will hold you responsible. Your customer will seek you out because you are the face of the brand. This is why hiring and working with the right dropshipping suppliers right from the beginning is so important.

- You don't have as much control over the creative process with dropshipping businesses. You won't be able to customize or personalize your packages because you're not the one handling it. The dropship supplier is. You have no control over how your packages and your products are presented, which eliminates the "personal touch" aspect that your customers can connect with.

- You can work closely with your supplier and work out an arrangement where you can work on personalizing your packages for that extra special touch, but this may end up costing you more money in the long run.

- There could be shipping issues that you need to contend with, especially when you opt to sell multiple products on your website. Dealing with a lot of dropshipping suppliers means you will have to deal with different shipping costs too, especially when some suppliers may charge more than others.

- Dropshipping competition rates are high because of what an attractive business model it is. Unless you're catering to a very specific niche audience, expect competition levels to be high and you will have to really compete to get your products to stand out.

- Miscommunication, cancellations, and backorders are just some of the many issues you may face when dealing with your suppliers. Keeping track of inventory may be tricky too, depending on whether you're selling one or multiple products.
- Profit margins are relatively low, so it might not be the best option for you if yours is a start-up business.
- There will be times when you face challenges such as the product being out of stock with the dropshipping supplier that you're working with. This can be an inconvenient problem, because it is frustrating for both the customer and for you. Having to coordinate between the your supplier and the customer to find a workable solution to the problem can be difficult to deal with, especially when you've got a difficult customer on your hands.

Knowing both the pros and cons will give you a good idea of what you can come to expect before you jump into this business with both feet. Due diligence matters, no matter what type of business you plan to get involved in.

Given the Pros and Cons, Is This a Profitable Business?
The profit margins that you can expect in the dropshipping business

can range anywhere from 15% to 45%. If you're selling luxury items or durables for example, your profit margins may be slightly higher. Some luxury goods can command up to 100% profit margins, depending on the items and the market you're selling to of course.

With dropshipping, the profit margin is going to depend upon getting the right supplier and the kind of niche market that you're servicing, and ad costs as well. The best way to ensure that your profit margins are higher is to try and source your profits directly from the manufacturer themselves, instead of going through a vendor or supplier. Cutting out the middleman means your profit margins have a chance of increasing. Especially once your business has gained some traction. Entering into a heavily saturated market may not be the best idea if profit is going to be your main concern.

Who Will Benefit Best From a Dropshipping Business Model?

Dropshipping is one of the best businesses to venture into if you're a first timer to the online business world. Or if you're someone who is looking to start their first business venture but looking for something relatively low-risk with low investment. Even if you currently own your own retail store, it can still be a good business to get into if you're looking to reach a wider market base.

The following types of entrepreneurs will get the most benefit out of the dropshipping business:

- **The Budgeter:** Those on a budget will love the dropshipping business model, because it is easily one of the least expensive business models out there in the online retail space. Especially when you don't have to purchase your inventory right from the beginning. If you're looking to keep your start-up costs low, this is the business model for you.

- **The Validator:** If you're the type of entrepreneur who needs high levels of product validation before you can be convinced to invest heavily in a product, dropshipping is a great way for you to test out the market with new products. That way, if you find it working for you, you can think about investing heavily into products that are doing well later on when you've got the capital for it.

- **The First-Timer:** Business can be daunting for a first-timer. The uncertainty of whether your business is going to make it, the high risk involved, the pressure of trying to get your business off the ground and how to gain market traction. It's a lot to take on, even selling online. Business is never easy for real success, which is why drop shipping offers the perfect solution logistically speaking; You get to ease into the business world without the high stakes risk while you test the market and understand how to sell online, what drives traffic, how to turn that traffic into sales and what it takes to optimize sales. This business model lets you learn the ropes before scaling your business even further so you can make smarter business investments moving forward.

Is there anyone who *doesn't benefit* from dropshipping? Yes, if you fall into any of the entrepreneurial categories below, then dropshipping may not be the business model that is going to suit your needs best:

- **You're An Entrepreneur Who Is Brand-Centric:** If you're an entrepreneur who is looking to build a brand around a product that you are selling, dropshipping is not the approach to take. Building a "brand" is something that is going to be difficult, challenging, and take a long time to do. However, the rewards that you stand to gain from it are well worth it. With dropshipping however, building a brand around your product is going to be difficult because of the other elements that go into the experience (such as not being able to personalize your delivery, packages, products etc like what was mentioned in the disadvantages section). If building a brand is going to be one of your primary concerns, you need to ask yourself whether dropshipping is really the approach that you want to take.

- **You're An Entrepreneur Who's Focused On the Margins:** Every entrepreneur is going to care about profit margins, but some entrepreneurs care more about it than others. The biggest problems with dropshipping is the low profit margins. Once you've dealt with the credit card fees, transaction fees, online services fees, e-commerce fees and other miscellaneous fees that you'll need to deal with, what you're going to be left with is a very small percentage of your profit that is left.

Chapter 2: Dropshipping Platforms Explained

Beginning a new business venture can be an exciting as much as it is challenging. With dropshipping, the excitement is just as real, especially when it is one of the lower-risk business models that you could opt to start with. The best part about this business model is the very low initial investment that you would need to fork out when compared with a lot of other business models.

Having dropshipping companies and suppliers to partner with, some of which even help to take care of the shipping aspect of the process for you, is one of the best things about this business. The right business partner is going to make a world of difference in the experience that you receive being part of the dropshipping world.

Current Dropshipping Platforms to Consider

When you're ready to start selling, there are a couple of dropshipping platforms that you could start looking at to consider your options:

- **Amazon FBA** - In case you're wondering what the FBA in Amazon FBA stands for, it is "Fulfilment by Amazon".

It is the perfect platform for the savvy entrepreneur who is keen on catering to a larger audience group. If this is you, then you're going to love this platform because it is well renown for its remarkably impressive scalability. What Amazon FBA can offer you is warehousing in addition to shipping services for your products. FBA in this instance, is offering you a unique approach, especially because Amazon is widely known for its product popularity.

The features that make this Amazon FBA option even more promising is that products are eligible for Amazon's shipping promotions. These promotions consists of options like Amazon Prime and Free Super Saver Shipping, and we all know how much a customer loves the free shipping options. Among the benefits that you stand to gain by using Amazon FBA include the fact that you're going to have plenty of time to focus on other aspects, like how to grow your business for example. That's because Amazon will take care of the packaging process for you, as well as the shipping process. Amazon is also well renown for its customer care services which are top notch. By using the Amazon FBA platform, you're going to be able to benefit from Amazon's massive pool of customers for even better sales results. Customers feel a lot more comfortable purchasing from

Amazon's site because of the returns and replacement policy that the platform has in place.

Amazon FBA takes its customer service very seriously, which is a definite perk in helping you maintain a loyal customer following, which is crucial for the survival of any business. Another benefit that you're going to get from relying on the Amazon brand name and image is that you get to sell your products for a slightly better profit margin than you would compared to other websites. That's the trust factor at play here, because customers know and recognize that they can trust Amazon, and therefore, are more comfortable paying the asking price than they would be shopping off other, less established sites where there is the fear that they may be cheated.

- **Shopify -** Shopify's popularity and power in the online dropshipping world is undisputed. Hosting approximate 500,000 dropshipping websites and e-commerce retail stores on its platform, Shopify is certainly a strong contender for dropshipping platforms which you could consider using. Oberlo was successfully acquired by this platform in 2016, and for if you're not familiar with Oberlo, it is a dropshipping plugin tool which allows product imports and makes order fulfilment and easier, simpler and hassle free process.

The reason for Shopify's popularity is that it is an extremely easy to use and user-friendly platform. Users simply need to sign up to its platform and create an account to begin adding products to your e-commerce store. Another benefit that comes with using this dropshipping platform is the pre-filled pages that Shopify provides, such as the About Us, Return and Privacy Policy, Shipping Calculator and even Shipping Information, all of which is available once you have set up a store on the platform. On top of that, this platform provides round the clock support 24/7. You can easily contact them through their chat support, or via email and phone if that is your preference. You could also easily find the help that you're looking for in Shopify's own official forum where other users of the platform come to share their knowledge, tips and tricks to help other users just like you.

One thing to note though, is that Shopify is a proprietary platform. This means that there won't be a lot of help available in community forums which are related to custom development. Shopify isn't a free platform either, and it comes with three pricing plan options for you to choose from that start from $29 and to all the way up to $299. When you've built up enough business momentum, you could even upgrade to Shopify's premium service, which is called Advanced Shopify. Shopify is home to many of the top dropshipping stores out there, like Pipcorn, Negative Underwear, Flat Spot and more.

- **Yahoo Store -** Just like Amazon, Yahoo has the added advantage of a reputable brand name behind it, should you choose to go with this platform. Yahoo Store works similar to platforms like Shopify, whereby you can quickly add products to your store with just a few simple clicks because it is easy to use. As an added bonus, Yahoo Store also accepts all sorts of payments and has the advantage of combining many shipping integrations. In terms of managing your inventory,

Yahoo's platform might come off as a little intimidating or difficult to use until you get the hang of it. Yahoo offers its users that peace of mind feature, with the promise that their platform works hard to take care of your business and to ensure that it is always safe and secure. If you require 24/7 support for the platforms that you use, then Yahoo is an option to consider, with their help and support being just a phone call or an email click away.

- **WooCommerce** - This platform is one of the most widely used in the e-commerce scene, used by people from all over the world. According to <u>Cloudways.com</u>, has a market share of more than 28% of the overall e-commerce stores. The reason why it has managed to command such a large market share is because it is a free platform which is easy to use, a major plus point since users are seeking a platform which is user friendly and easy to navigate. No one wants the hassle of dealing with a platform that is complicated and too time-consuming to figure out, that is just off-putting. With WooCommerce, all you need to do is simply install it with a single click, so users don't necessary have to be tech savvy to still be able to reap the benefits of this dropshipping platform. The site comes with simple GUI interface, so easy that even a new user to the site will be able to instantly grasp the concept of how it works. The WooCommerce platform is built on one of the most favorite blogger platforms out there, which is WordPress, and because of that, you'll be able to easy install many of its multiple add-ons for free.

Another major benefit that comes with using the WooCommerce platform is that it has a widespread community of developers and designers who are constantly actively working to promote this platform. If you ever need a lot of material on how to go about your installation, or even require support at any stage during the process, help is easily available. Thanks to its popularity, WooCommerce is home to approximately millions of other e-commerce stores, which means you'll be able to source for many of the famous websites like Ripley's Believe It Or Not, Singer, All Black and even Weber Grills.

- **Oberlo** - Bought over by Shopify in 2016, Oberlo has cemented a reputation for itself as one of the world' leading marketplaces where users can come to find the products that they want to sell online in their Shopify e-commerce stores. Oberlo's platform works to help facilitate Shopify's dropshipping aspect by connecting the suppliers and merchants, who will then work to ship the products which have been ordered directly to the consumers. One of the best features about Oberlo's platform is its modern and visually appealing user interface. It has a tight-knit integration with Shopify's platform, which is a definite advantage but the downside that also comes with this option is that this platform only works with Shopify stores. There is also no shipment, or monitoring for order fulfilment with this option, but they do offer a easy, one-click import for your AliExpress products. Oberlo does have the option of signing up for a free account, but the drawback with that one is that you're only limited to 500 products on your platform and about 50 orders per month, which will put a definite dent in the amount of profits that you can receive. With the paid option, it can start from as low as $29.90 per month and go as high as $79.90 per month.

- **BigCommerce** - As an e-commerce platform that is hosted, BigCommerce has done well for itself in claiming its fair share of the market. Hosting approximately 50,000 websites for small businesses, and about 2000 and more enterprise companies, BigCommerce is a contender against other platforms to be sure. What makes this platform popular among its users is the simple to use user interface and how quickly they can set up their a store. Compared to other platforms like Shopify for example, BigCommerce is easily more affordable since it does not charge its users any transaction fees. On top of that, it offers the benefit of unlimited discounts for its staff, along with other prominent features including offering the same type of customer support system that Shopify does. You can reach out and contact support through its forums, emails, chats and phone calls. As a testament to its popularity, BigCommerce is known for hosting multiple big name companies, including the likes to Toyota, Nine Line Apparel and Marucci Sports. Prices for this platform start from as low as $29 and go up to $250.

Tips and Tricks for Success

Tips and tricks are great, especially for newcomers to this industry, because it can quickly help you learn the ropes and navigate your way around to speed up your success rate. Faster, better, results in less time is music to the ears of many entrepreneurs. These aren't shortcuts, but simply insightful advice into how to work *smarter* instead of harder.

- **Keeping Your Eyes On the Prize** - Your main goal with starting any business is to make a profit, and therefore, you should never lose focus of that fact. Avoid being tempted, distracted or carried away by the so call "must haves" for your website, or be too caught up in having flashy graphics or content which is far too long-winded for your consumers to maintain an interest in. The idea is to keep your sight simple yet attractive enough to keep your target audience interested. They should instantly be able to navigate your site without any problems. A website which is far to complicated is going to drive them away, and in doing so, drive away your chance of making a profit.

- **Don't Forget About SEO** - This should be an integral part of your marketing strategies. Yes, there is going to be marketing involved, even with a business model like dropshipping. Don't believe it when they tell you that SEO is dead. **It is not**, so long as keywords are still used to search for anything and everything on the internet. You need to use SEO wisely not only on your website but also on your social media which is from content, titles, tags, image tags, descriptions.

- **See Things From the Customers Perspective** - You're going to have to think like a customer and put yourself in their shoes. If you were to go to a website where you would like to make a purchase, what do you expect to see? What sort of buying process is going to make you feel happy and satisfied about making a purchase? What are the features that you personally like from some of the websites that you have purchased form in the past? All these factors are going to come into play in making your own website as perfect as possible for your customer experience. Give the customers what they want and they will be more likely to keep returning for more.

Encourage Product Reviews - Don't be afraid of product reviews, because this is the weapon that you need to encourage other users who have not purchased from your website before to *want to buy from you.* Honest product reviews help to convince new customers that they are making the right choice in choosing to purchase form your platform instead of your competitors. The best way for any customer to know that the products that they are purchasing are value for money is by reading reviews. Customers will click on products that have higher ratings and the likelihood of them purchasing it is if has good reviews and high ratings.

Chapter 3: Sourcing Your Suppliers

One beginning your dropshipping business, one of the most important aspects that you need to focus on is the finding the right suppliers. It is also important to distinguish between a supplier and a retailer too. Your suppliers are going to be crucial key contact points, because they are the ones who are going to provide your customers with the products that they ordered from your website.

What You Need to Do Before Contacting Your Suppliers

First, you need to work on a list of suppliers that you would like to work with before you attempt to contact them. After you've craved out your list though, there are still several things that you would need to do before contacting your suppliers (contact will be the last step of the process). To ensure you are successful when you approach the suppliers that you want to increase your chances of scoring a working relationship with them, here's what you need to do:

- **Get Yourself Legalized** - Wholesalers will need proof that your business is legit before they can even begin to consider a working relationship with you. Legitimate wholesalers, especially, take this very seriously. If you're not legalized, you will not be allowed to open a business account with them, which means that you must get your business legally incorporated with all the right licenses, permits and documentation that you need to show as proof to these wholesalers.

- **Be Professional** - Suppliers will be getting a lot of inquires on a regular basis from retailers, and these queries take up a lot of their time. Understandably, it is frustrating for them when after all that, no order ends up being placed with them. Therefore, before you approach them, you need to know that a great business plan alone is only going to get you so far with these suppliers. They are going to need to see more than that from you. Don't expect suppliers to empathize with you, you need to appear professional and serious about your business for them to take you seriously. While they will be more than happy to help you set up a dropshipping account, don't expect too many favors from them, they are still running a business at the end of the day. If all you're doing is taking up far too much of their time without making any real progress, word is going to spread among other suppliers and you might find it challenging to find someone who is willing to work with you.

- **Be Credible** - Building on the point above, you must also build a credible reputation for yourself, along with a professional one. Don't jump into making special requests and asking for favors right away when you haven't proved yourself yet, especially if you are a newbie to this industry.

Build credibility by being definite about your business planes, your launch dates, quantities, shipping dates in as much detail as possible instead of providing vague answers like "perhaps or maybe". Your objective is to convince suppliers that dealing with you is going to be a good investment of their time and their business. Communicating your professional successes in the past because it can help with your dealings with a supplier.

And now, it's time to pick up the phone and talk to them. While email is the preferred method of communication for many these days, the old fashion phone call is a much better prospect when it comes to securing a business deal or partnership with your supplier. The advantage of making a direct phone call is that any issues faced can be ironed out on the spot as opposed to waiting days for an email response which could go back and forth for some time. Sending follow-up emails after the phone call is good for keeping the relationship and the rapport going, but in the beginning, you should consider starting with a phone call right away. Suppliers always have people calling them, including people new to the business, so you don't have to worry about being the only one doing this. More often than not, you'll get a sales representative that is more than happy to answer your questions, because you are a potential client too at the end of the day.

Where to Find Wholesale Suppliers

When it comes to sourcing your suppliers, there are several strategies which you can employ to find the right suppliers for your business:

- **Contacting the Manufacturer Directly -** Directly making contact with the manufacturer is one of the best ways to go about sourcing who you can potentially work with. Once you're already sure of the products that you intend to sell on your website, you can start sourcing for the suppliers who are handling the kind of products that you want to sell. Picking up the phone and calling them, speaking to them and asking the questions that you need to know is one of the best approaches to take to directly find out the information that you need. Prepare a list of questions ahead of time so you can carry on a professional conversation over the home in an effective manner. Assuming that all your questions are answered satisfactorily inquire about opening an account with them if you think you would like to work with them.

- **A Quick Search on Google -** One of the best places to source what you're looking for. However, you need to still conduct extensive research and look into which sources are credible. There will be thousands of search results showing up when you type in what you're looking for in the search engines, but not all suppliers are going to be what you're looking for. Some wholesalers may not even appear in the top 10 search results because they may not be actively promoting their business. You should conduct extensive research and look into a supplier that you do like, because some websites may be outdated too. A quick tip when searching on Google for your suppliers is to use modifiers. This means use keywords which include "warehouse", "reseller" or "bulk" in your search terms.

- **Going to Trade Shows** - Meeting and networking directly with manufacturers and wholesalers who attend these trade shows is another great approach to take when you're sourcing for suppliers that you can work with. This method works great only if you have picked your niche and the product that you want to sell within that niche. Networking and meeting them in person let's you see who you will be working with, and you'll be able to determine for yourself if you'll be able to create a great working relationships with them. Meeting face to face also helps to build real business partnerships.

- **Going Through Directories** - Many directories use a screening process to legitimize their suppliers and ensure they try are genuine wholesalers, so this is another good (and more importantly, safe) approach to take to source for legitimate suppliers. A directory is supplier database is another way of scoring a good selection of suppliers based on market or niche. These lists are certainly helpful, especially if you're pressed for time and don't have the necessary resources to do the extensive research and due diligence that is needed to find credible sources on your own. Especially in the beginning when you're just starting to find your footing. Supplier directories prove to be a convenient method of quickly searching for and browsing a large number of potential suppliers.

- **Via Oberlo -** If you want the convenience of easily importing your products from the suppliers to your online store, *and* be able to ship it directly to your customers after that, Oberlo could be something to look into. Here, you will be able to fulfil your orders automatically, customize your products and even conduct pricing automation too.

- **Sourcing Suppliers From Your Competition -** As a last resort, what you can do is source for the same suppliers as your competitors. If you were to make a purchase from your competitor, there will be a return address on the package that you receive. A quick search on Google will reveal which shipper the original address belongs too. From there, you will be able to contact the supplier to find out if you can work with them too.

How Do I Know When I've Found a Good Supplier?

Working with the right supplier is going to be crucial to the success of your dropshipping business. Suppliers play a very important role, without them your customers are not going to be able to get the products that they've ordered from you. While it is no problem to source for a supplier, finding a *good supplier* is the challenge. When conducting your search for the right suppliers who are going to be the best fit for you and your business needs, take the following into consideration:

- **A Good Supplier Has Dedicated Support Staff** - A good supplier is going to take their job seriously, and as such, they will have a group of dedicated support representatives because they know it is important to have the right "face" for the business. Suppliers who are professional also have a sales rep that is equipped with the knowledge of industry needs and they are also trained with the know-how of the industry and the product lines that they are dealing with. They also take the necessary steps to ensure that their staff will be with you every step of the way, guiding you throughout the entire process. Be wary of suppliers who don't take the trouble to assign you with a specific sales representative to help you, because often you'll find that these suppliers will be the one that cause you more issues and problems than necessary. They may also take much longer to resolve an issue, and you may end up having to go through a roundabout method just to get your issue resolved. An unnecessary hassle, and one that you want to do your best to avoid. Having a single supplier contact who deals exclusively with your case for solving your issues is really important and crucial.

- **They Are Located in A Central Area -** Having a supplier that is easy to access is going to make your life a lot easier. In business, it is all about location, location, location. With dropshipping businesses, it works the same way when sourcing for the right suppliers. Why a centrally located supplier makes such a difference is because a central location will enable packages to be shipped and delivered within 2 to 3 business days. Suppliers located at coastal areas often take a week or more to get orders shipped and delivered. If fast shipping is a priority for your business, ensuring that your customers get their orders in a timely fashion, then look for suppliers who are going to be centrally located. Conveniently located suppliers also allow you to consistently promote your customers faster delivery times, enabling you to save more money on fees and having a happy customer. Suppliers located at coastal areas for example, often take a week or more to get orders shipped and delivered, so that might not be the best fit for you if fast shipping is a priority.

- **They're OK Accepting Orders Via Email -** Having to call and manually place your orders through the website can be a very tedious and time consuming task. If efficiency is what you're after, look for suppliers who are perfectly fine with accepting and processing orders via emails. A supplier who is professional makes the email order process a seamless approach, saving you a lot of time and effort in the long run.

- **They Are Efficient** - Efficiency is everything in the business world. When one party does not behave in an organized and efficient manner, the whole system can break down, causing unnecessary delays in order shipments and fulfilments. This is something every dropshipping business should aim to avoid, and if you find a supplier who displays attributes of being efficient, professional and organized, these are the suppliers that you want to be working with. Having competent staff and excellent systems is like having a well-tuned and functional website. It reduces errors, saves time and keeps both parties happy. Incompetent staff results in botched orders and unhappy customers. Unhappy customers can mean the death of your business, because without them, you wouldn't have a business to begin with in the first place. The issue here it's difficult to know how competent a supplier is without actually using it. This is why reading reviews are important. Look for suppliers who ship out their orders in a timely manner, the quality of their packaging, the efficiency of providing an invoice and tracking information once the order has shipped out, and how efficient their ordering process is for signs of a well-organized supplier.

Making Payments To Your Suppliers

Suppliers generally accept two forms of payment methods, which are either via credit card, or Net terms. Credit card payment is usually the preferred payment for suppliers especially if you are new and establishing a presence in the industry. Once you have a thriving business, credit cards are still the best option as they are more convenient especially for making online payments. Net terms on an invoice is another common way to pay suppliers. When using this method, you are usually given a certain period to pay off the supplier. For example, if you have a "net 30" terms, this means you have exactly 30 days from the purchase date to pay your supplier. You can do this either by check or a bank draw.

Chapter 4: Niche Selection and Order Fulfilment

Now that you know how to go about looking for suppliers for your dropshipping business, the next step of the process is to find your niche in dropshipping. Once you've established your niche, it becomes easier to fulfil the orders that come in so your business can build a sustainable momentum that keeps it going. Hopefully with an increase in profits over time, if you play your cards right.

It may seem strange that you would need to find a niche market in an online world filled with endless possibilities, many of which you no doubt would like to be involved in, but there's a reason for it. Finding a niche can seem overwhelming, to narrow your focus to a specific selection instead of broadening it for more potential, but if you find the right niche and work it to your advantage, this has a much better opportunity of bringing in more profits for your business.

With a niche market, you get to build a reputation for yourself. Provide excellent service every time and the regular customers within this niche will come to know your name. Provide a service which pleases enough customers and your reputation will start to build. Once the customers in this niche begin to associate you with great service and great quality, it won't be long before they become repeat customers.

Repeat customers are what every business strives for, because these repeat customers ensure a steady flow of business. A dropshipping business model may operate different from other business models, but at its very core, it is still a *business*. A business that wants to survive must be strong enough and good enough to capture a loyal customer following. This helps to ensure that you don't constantly have to scramble trying to figure out how to drive your sales and keep your business alive.

How to Select the Right Niche Market for Your Dropshipping Business

To select the right niche market, there are a couple of strategies which you could employ:

- **Research, research and more research -** There's a lot of research that is going to go into this stage of your business, but it has to be done. You need to research, compare and evaluate the current dropshipping trends and what you have to work with. When researching prices of items for example, look at several platforms instead of focusing on just one. For example, research current trends on Amazon and eBay, but don't make those the only platforms that you are looking at.

Broaden your search to include different types of niches. Look at the higher-priced bracket items, and compare that to the lower bracket items. Compare and evaluate the dropshipping trends that you are observing on this platform. What is selling well and what isn't. What trends seem to be doing well and why. Even when you're sourcing for suppliers, request a price quote from a few suppliers and then compare shipping quotes from customs brokers and storage capacities for a product too. The more areas of your business that your research covers the better.

- **Brainstorm for Ideas:** Brainstorming has always been one of the most effective approaches to trying to come up with new ideas and solutions to problems. In everyday life and in business. This technique is now going to come in handy towards helping you find the perfect niche market for your business too. Start brainstorming ideas for a niche. Talk to like-minded business friends who could give you some other insight, or perhaps even more ideas, maybe even have a brainstorming session or two with them. If you know anyone else who is involved in the dropshipping industry too, try and talk to them and see what advice they can help you out with. Talk to friends and family who are supportive, because they too may be able to come up with some pretty good ideas that you could work with. Brainstorming sessions should be done as often as you feel it is necessary. Set a time for it, block out your calendar for a couple of hours to commit to this brainstorming session and focus entirely on that. If you're doing this business alone, invite other like-minded friends or family members to join in your session. If you've got a business partner in with you on this venture, then brainstorm with them. Write down everything you know about possible niche options, list them down in order of competition, loyalty, pricing, returns and more. Compare and contrast which niche is going to give you the best returns and you may have your answer in front of you on those pieces of paper where you just poured out all your ideas.

- **Thinking Like a Marketer -** It may seem like the odd choice, but selling expensive items is one of the best things you can do with your dropshipping business. Think about this - the average profit that gets made for dropshipping is about 20% of the total sales that you make. Which means that you're making a 20% profit from an item which you sell. If you're selling something expensive which is worth let's say, $1000, the profit that you stand to make would be $200, which is 20% of that item. Now, compare that to if you were to sell an item for $10 for example, where your 20% profit would only be $2. Naturally, the profit from the more expensive items definitely looks better. Look at your current competitors online and what they are selling the same items for. Not only do you have to observe what your current competition is doing, you would also need to identify the potential future competition that might crop up. Remember, business is a fast changing environment, so keeping abreast of your competition is going to be something you need to consistently work on.

- **Searching on Amazon** - As one of the biggest retailers in the world, Amazon sells just about everything on its platform. Thanks to the presence and reputation it has built for itself over the years, this is now one of the best platforms that you could use at your disposal to find a profitable niche market for your own dropshipping business. Searching for a potential niche on Amazon is easy. All you would need to do is to simply click the "All" tab which is located on the left side of the main search bar and from there, you will easily find a list of categories which you can select from. Simply find a niche category that grabs your interest, click the "Go" button and wait for the new page to pop up. On the left hand side of that page, you will then see the option to select a "sub-niche" category and by clicking on that link, you will be able to view even *more* specific sub-niches. It's a great platform to source for potential options, and the best part is you will be able to view which products are doing and selling well. Searching for best selling products is easy to, all you would need to do is click on the "Best Sellers" tab from the navigation bar and there you go.

Passion vs Income

This is the toughest choice for anyone thinking about doing business, weighing your passion against your profits. Of course, everyone wants to make as much money as possible, but at the same time, you need to think about doing something that you love, something that you're passionate about so you can go at it long term.

In the eternal question about passion versus income and which you should go for, that would really depend on you at the end of the day. For some people, starting this dropshipping business is a way to work on doing a business that they love, while for others, they may be motivated to get into this line for work for the extra money that they want to see coming into their bank accounts. For the latter group, they don't mind what they sell as long as they are selling something.

But what if your passion doesn't bring in as big a profit as some other dropshipping niche market categories? Well, that's where the balancing act is going to come in, where you try to balance out pursuing a business that is your passion while trying to generate a sustainable profit coming in at the same time. Even though profits may be a big concern, it is equally important *not to overlook* the passion part. **You _must have an interest in the items that you are selling, this point cannot be stress enough_**, if you don't, you will not have the motivation to see yourself through the challenging trial periods to success and profits. This is the same process in any business.

In the earlier chapters, it was mentioned how challenging running a business can be, **and dropshipping is no different**(experienced business owners know this), if you don't have a love for what you're selling, it will be very hard for you to find the drive to keep on going on the days which challenge you the most. When you put your love and everything that you've got into what you're selling, it is going to show, even if it is done online. Your customers are going to see it in the kind of service you provide, the customer support and the way that you take great care in ensuring your products get delivered in the best possible condition. The follow up after-sales care is the one that is going to make a difference. If you don't love what you're doing, the only thing you're going to care about is the money at the end of the day, and that is not going to be good enough for your customers.

While passion certainly does play a major role in you choosing to go into the dropshipping business, a profitable niche is the one that is going to keep your bank balance looking happy and putting a smile on your face. To find a balance between your passion and the profits that you want to make, there's several questions you need to ask yourself.

First, let's determine the level of passion that you have for the business:

- What are the websites that you frequent the most in your spare time?
- What kind of groups and interests do your follow actively on your social media channels?
- What types of stores or products do you like to purchase most often online?
- Is there a certain type of product that you actively like to purchase because it makes you happy? Or brings you joy?
- If you had a certain amount of money to spend on a product - any product - that you *want but don't necessarily need,* what would you choose to spend that money on and why?

The answers that you've given above will provide you with some idea about the kind of products that you're passionate in. Now, weigh that against the profits that you want to make. To do that, you need to research:

- What products or product trends are the most popular right now? Is the product within an area of your interest?
- Which products are drawing in the biggest profit margins from dropshipping? Is that product within an area of your interest?
- What types of products are your competitors selling that are doing really well right now? Are those products within an area of your interest?

If there is a vast difference between the products and ignite your passion and the kind of products which draw in the biggest profit, then perhaps you need to aim for an in between balance of trying to target an evergreen niche instead.

An evergreen niche is a product that would generally do well for most retailers because it is a product range that is not going to disappear or fade in popularity anytime soon. Categories of these products include; fashion, beauty, and household products which consumers need monthly, for example. Select the trending evergreen niche that is going to be the best match for your area of passion so that you will be able to draw in healthy profit levels regularly, while still maintaining an interest for what you're doing.

Other Tools to Help You Find Your Niche

Finding your niche these days is much easier when everything is available online. Other tools which you could use to help you narrow down on a niche that you can start venturing into include:

- Google Trends
- Facebook Search
- Compete.com, which is a great platform for sourcing the latest market demand
- Social Mention, for real time social media search and analysis

Fulfilling Your Dropshipping Orders

Dropshipping is not a product, it is a *service* which you are providing. The very critical role that you are playing in the dropshipping scenario is to ensure that the products which get ordered through your website are shipped out in a timely manner and that your customer is getting what they want.

Ensuring that the order gets fulfilled is the job that you now have to ensure gets done. The ordering process is simple enough:

- The customer places an order through your site.
- Once the payment and order has been confirmed, the

customer will get an email notifying them of a successful order which has been placed.

- The details of this order will then get sent to the supplier.
- Once the supplier has confirmed that the items are in stock, the wholesaler will the box and ship the items directly to the customer.
- Although the supplier is the one that ships out the order, it is your details which are going to appear on the return address that gets sent to the customer, including your company's logo and return details.
- Once the shipment has been finalized and sent out successfully, the supplier will then email you a copy of the invoice with the tracking number and all the relevant details. Depending on the supplier that you're using and stock availability, some suppliers will ship out products within a few hours of receiving the order, which will give you the advantage of advertising same-day shipping or 24-hour shopping.
- Once you have received the shipment tracking number from your supplier, you will need to send these details to the customer. You can do this either directly via email, or automated through the built in feature on your e-commerce site's interface.
- Once the product has been shipped out, the payment received and collected, and the customer has been

notified accordingly, only *then* is your order considered fulfilled and complete.

Your profit from this order fulfilment will depend on the difference which was charged to your customer and how much you had to pay your supplier. In this entire cycle, the dropshipper is going to remain complete invisible to the customer throughout the order fulfilment process. You will be the contact point for the customer should they need to reach out to you for anything. If they receive the wrong order, you will be their point of contact, not the supplier. Your role is to merely coordinate with your supplier to ensure all the order details get fulfilled the way that they should.

To your customer, the "dropshipper" does not exist in this sales scenario. It is just a transaction between you and them. Therefore, in the order fulfilment process, it is going to be entirely your responsibility to ensure the success of the sale. You will be doing everything from advertising on your website, marketing your products, providing the necessary customer service needed and more.

Chapter 5: Online Advertising

Living in the digital age has awarded business with many advantages. One of them being the ability to advertise online as well as sell online. Thanks to how much the internet has advanced the world as we know it today, dropshipping has become a business model which is immensely popular, especially among the millennial generation.

Dropshipping's biggest allure lies in the fact that you don't need to physically stock up on these products that you want to sell, that you can start selling with even limited funds as long as you have a website platform which has been optimized for e-commerce, and that dropshipping is one of the very few business models which effectively cuts your business cost in half. By saving your funds in several areas, you are not effectively able to channel it into the sources that do matter, such as online advertising for example. Because without advertising, how will people come to know about your e-commerce site?

Why Online Advertising for Your Dropshipping Business Is Important

The internet is a fast moving environment. You only need to scroll through your social media channels to see just how fast moving these platforms are. Items and newsfeeds get refreshed an updated with new content in mere minutes. If a business does not do everything it possibly can to stand out from the rest of its competitors, it won't be long before that business gets drowned out by everyone else. In fact if you are not publishing content on your Facebook page regular Facebook will de-publish it automatically.

Dropshipping, because of the many benefits that it offers, attracts thousands of hopeful entrepreneurs just like yourself. With such high levels of competition, you want to be doing everything that you can to make sure that your site gets noticed. Advertising is one of the ways to go about doing this. If you're selling clothing items for example, you can be sure that there will be hundreds if not thousands of other e-commerce sites just like yours selling the exact same thing.

You need to stand out. That is the only way that your business is going to survive this highly competitive environment. As mentioned in the previous chapters, selecting your niche and an area that you have a vast knowledge or experience in is going to help. This will make it significantly easier for you to keep going because it is easier for you to market something that you know, or something that you're passionate about. You *must* have a passion for the products that you are selling with your dropshipping business. A businessman or businesswoman never starts a business with something that they are not passionate about. Not only can it be a costly mistake, it can be a detrimental one. In times of challenge, it is your passion and your love for what you do that keeps you going, and you need this aspect even in the dropshipping business world.

What Sort of Advertising Should I Focus On?

The beauty of online advertising is that there is no one way to go about doing it. Advertising digitally, compared to conventional advertising methods of the past, leaves a lot more room for creativity. With various editing tools available online, your creativity is only limited by what you can do.

When thinking about online advertising for your dropshipping business, here's are some areas that you want to focus on shining the spotlight:

- Highlight what is unique or special about your product
- How your products are going to solve a need or want that your customer has
- Advertise promotions and special offers or exclusive discounts
- Advertise any competitions or giveaways that you are running on your platform
- Market your content across all your available social media channels

- Advertise what makes you different from your competitor. Is it the low shipping cost? The money back guarantee? The better customer care experience?

Your customers want to know what is special about your product. They want to know why they should be buying from you and not someone else. They want to know what's in it for them if they were to purchase from you instead of your competitor.

You would also need to target your advertising efforts towards your niche market, because these are the people with the biggest potential who are likely to purchase your products. A customer is unlikely to become a repeat buyer unless your product is something they absolutely need to have in their lives. Something they cannot live without. Retaining your customer is the key to ensuring continuous success with your e-commerce site, and this the element that you need to remember when crafting out your advertising campaigns.

What You Need to Do Before Advertising Online

Look at what your competitors are doing. That is very important. Who are your biggest competitors and how are they going about their advertising efforts. Among your biggest competitors will be much bigger, established household names like Amazon for example. If you are selling products which are similar to your competitors, how they are advertising their products? What can you do to make it better?

With online advertising, it is about what you can do to capture your customer's attention. How are you going to make your products so appealing that they simply have to pause and take a second look, perhaps even buy from you if you conduct your advertising campaigns just right.

Why Online Advertising Is Better Than Print for Your Dropshipping Business?

Think your dropshipping business doesn't need advertising? Think again. It may be small, but not small enough to overlook the advertising aspect altogether. Why online advertising proves to be the better approach is simply because everything is going digital these days, and also because dropshipping is an *online business platform.* therefore, what better way to advertise your business than on the platform on which it is built?

While print advertising still exists, it is slowly being pushed aside and overshadowed by the popularity of online advertisements. You will see these print ads occasionally here and there, but rarely are they able to grab the attention of the customer the way online ads do.

Here are several other reasons why online advertising is much better than traditional print advertising for your dropshipping business:

- **The Mobility That These Ads Have** - Your customers today will be connected through a number of devices. Anything from smartphones, to tablets, laptops and desktops. As long as they have got an internet connection, they are able to connect to anyone, any business at any time or location. Nearly everywhere you go these days, you will rarely find someone who is without at least a smartphone. In fact, a survey conducted by *Periscope by McKinney* in 2018 discovered that at least 70% of the people that they surveyed were doing at least some form of online shopping, purchasing consumer packaged goods mostly. Online shopping has gained traction over the years because of the convenience that it offers, and with more and more customers turning to online shopping platforms, this spells massive potential for dropshipping business owners to tap into if they want to grab onto that market share. We live in a society that is constantly on the go, which makes online advertising and its mobility ability the *only way* to go.

- **Online Advertising Gives You a Global Reach -** Print advertisements are limited by many things, one of them being the demographic reach that it can provide. With online advertising however, the world is literally at your fingertips. From the moment you hit the "publish" button, anyone with an internet connection from anywhere in the world will be able to access your content. Billions of people will be able to see and view your products. More importantly, they have access to *buy* your products if they like what they see. This vast potential for reaching global markets alone is a very sound and convincing reason why your business needs to start advertising online (if you're not already doing so).

- **Measuring Your Results Is Much Easier -** While you can measure your results with print advertising too, the availability of several types of online marketing tools these days make it easy for you to choose *the best tool* that is going to suit your business needs best. Search Engine Optimization or SEO, is an especially good way to measure the effectiveness of how your online ad campaigns are doing. That's because SEOs measure not just the quality of your content and whether you're using the right keywords or not, but it also evaluate your backlinks, traffic, rankings and even your indexation metrics. The latter's metrics is the one that is responsible for determining whether your website is being picked up by this search engines based on the keywords or key phrases that you've used. If you want your business to get noticed, SEO optimization for your content is a must, and tracking your success is much easier when you choose to advertise online. This is something you can't do quite as effectively with print advertising.

- **Identifying Where Your Target Audience Is Easier** - Another benefit to advertising online is that, with a little bit of research (okay, maybe a lot of research), you're able to identify where your niche audience groups spend most of their time. Is it on Facebook? Instagram? Twitter or Pinterest? Perhaps even LinkedIn or SnapChat? Wherever your niche audience is hanging out, that is where you need to be. It is easy to for your ad campaigns to immediately hit the right audience group, once you know where to look and where to aim for. That is just one of the many ways in which the online world has drastically change the marketing and advertising world as we know it for the better.

- **It Is Cost Effective** - Keeping in line with the cost-effectiveness theme which surrounds the dropshipping business model, another reason why online advertising is a hands-down winner compared to its alternative is because of the cost effectiveness value attached to it. Facebook Ads for example, is one of the best online advertising platforms available today because of the unmatched low-cost rates that it offers. Not only is it easy to use, it is one of the cheapest advertising tools that every business is tapping into these days. On top of that, it is one of the most popular social media platforms in existence, boasting a user base of 2.32 billion monthly active users, according to <u>Zephoria Digital Marketing</u>'s most recent statistics as of December 2018. This means you have the potential to reach 2.32 billion customers, many of whom may be keen on what you have to sell. Let that number sink in for a minute. And this is just *one* social media platform.

- **Your Content Is Constantly Exposed** - As long as your content is not deleted from your platform, it is out there for the world to see. Anytime, anywhere, day, night or weekend, all your customers need to do is head to your e-commerce site to shop and find what they're looking for. This is what your online advertisements are here to remind them about. That everything they're looking for and more is available on your site, and as long as they are surfing the internet, your ads will be there to remind them about that fact. This constant exposure is akin to your ad campaigns being run 24/7, even while you sleep, because somewhere else in the world, someone is awake and surfing the net for what you are selling.

Final Thoughts

Despite the popularity of online advertising, that doesn't mean that print media is entirely dead altogether. Some forms of print media still exists, and they do work depending on how your business uses them. Supermarkets for example, still rely on print media to print their weekly catalogue promotions and these are still being well received by customers who frequent the supermarkets.

Bigger health-related brands and companies are still advertising in selected magazines that they know are of specific interest to their targeted audience. Print ads are still around because they do work to some extent, but because the dropshipping business is primarily an online business model, print advertising may not be the most effective approach to take in this context.

Ultimately, online advertising is still the best approach to take to advertising your dropshipping business because the benefits that it brings - compared to that of print ads - is unmatched. The digital world has plenty of opportunities, options and choices for just about every business type, and all you need to do is to find the avenue that works best for you and work from there.

List of References

https://www.cloudways.com/blog/woocommerce-market-share/

https://www.cloudways.com/blog/best-ecommerce-platform-for-dropshipping-business/

https://trends.google.com/trends/?geo=US

http://inboundly.com.au/5-tools-for-finding-niche-online/

http://www.socialmention.com/

https://www.shopify.com/guides/dropshipping/supply-chain-and-fulfillment-process

https://www.inc.com/peter-roesler/new-research-reveals-more-consumers-are-shopping-online-for-everyday-items.html

https://zephoria.com/top-15-valuable-facebook-statistics/

https://www.affordablewebdesign.com/5-reasons-why-internet-marketing-is-better-than-print-advertising/

Summary

Dropshiping has been around a long time, it was widely available when regular mail order businesses were the main business model pre-Internet days, and is not the de facto for "Online" mail order businesses, nothing has changed, just the tools, accessibility and cost now is SIGNIFICANTLY cheaper and faster to set up a real business. You can literally set up your website and elements in 2 days, select a suppliers, set up ad campaigns and be off and running in under 3 full days of effort, think about that. <u>What used to take 2-6 months of logistical processes, scheduling print and magazine ads and planning can now be done in a few days!</u>

You've now been equipped with everything that you need to begin your foray into the world of dropshipping and begin reaping all the benefits that come with being your own boss. Of course, there are challenges that go along with it, but that's what makes it interesting. This book is just the tiny iceberg to your new venture, keep learning as the digital landscape is changing very FAST EVERY DAY, so you need to stay up to date, especially with online ads.